HALEAKALĀ NATIONAL PARK

A TRUE BOOK

by

David Petersen

Children's Press®
A Division of Scholastic Inc.

New York Toronto London Auckland Sydney
Mexico City New Delhi Hong Kong
Danbury, Connecticut

Hikers on
a trail in
Haleakalā
National
Park

Subject Consultant
Sharon Ringsven
Supervisory Park Ranger
Haleakalā National Park

**Visit Children's Press® on the
Internet at:
http://publishing.grolier.com**

Library of Congress Cataloging-in-Publication Data

Petersen, David, 1946–
   Haleakalā National Park / by David Petersen
     p. cm. — (A true book)
   Includes bibliographical references and index.
   ISBN 0-516-21666-X (lib. bdg.)   0-516-27318-3 (pbk.)
   1. Haleakalā National Park (Hawaii)—Juvenile literature. 2. Maui
(Hawaii)—Description and travel—Juvenile literature. [1. Haleakalā
National Park (Hawaii) 2. National parks and reserves.] I. Title. II. Series.
DU628.H25 P48 2001
996.9'21—dc21   00-030697

GROLIER
PUBLISHING

Contents

The Legend of Haleakalā 5

How the Islands Began 9

Maui, Island of Volcanoes 14

Life in Haleakalā 22

The First People 32

Visiting Haleakalā 38

Fast Facts 43

To Find Out More 44

Important Words 46

Index 47

Meet the Author 48

Hawaiian Islands

Kaua'i

O'ahu

PACIFIC OCEAN

Maui

N
W   E
S

HAWAI'I

Haleakalā
National
Park

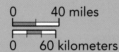
0   40 miles

0   60 kilometers

Hawai'i

HALEAKALĀ NATIONAL PARK

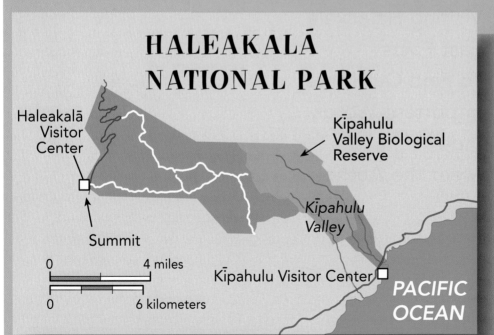

Haleakalā
Visitor
Center

Kīpahulu
Valley Biological
Reserve

Summit

Kīpahulu
Valley

0   4 miles

0   6 kilometers

Kīpahulu Visitor Center

PACIFIC
OCEAN

The Legend of Haleakalā

Haleakalā National Park covers about two-thirds of Maui, the second largest of the eight main Hawaiian Islands. Haleakalā (hah-lay-ah-kah-LAH), the mountain that gives the park its name, means "House of the Sun" in Hawaiian. An ancient legend tells the story behind that name.

Long ago, Hawai'i was not the warm and sunny place it is today. Back then, the days were short and cool. Māui, the young god who lived on the island that now bears his name, knew the days were short because the sun was lazy— rising late, and racing across the sky so it could rest again.

One night, Māui took a rope to the top of Haleakalā, and

A hiker enjoying a
sunny day in the park

waited for the dawn. When the sun began to rise, Māui roped in all the sunbeams and tied them to a tree. The sun realized that it was trapped and begged Māui to set it free. Māui made the sun promise, from that day on, to creep very slowly across the sky. The sun kept its promise, and Hawai'i now enjoys long, sunny days. This is how Haleakalā got its name—House of the Sun.

How the Islands Began

As famous and popular as Hawai'i is today, it remains the most remote group of islands in the world. The nearest continent, North America, is 2,400 miles (3,860 kilometers) away. Volcanoes formed all the islands of Hawai'i,

The Hawaiian Islands

including Maui. Volcanoes are mountains made of lava rock, or volcanic rock.

The Earth's hard, thin outer crust is made up of about thirty huge pieces, called tectonic plates. Pressure deep within our planet causes the plates to move around. The plates move slowly on a layer of hot rock beneath the crust.

The melting rock found deep inside the Earth is called magma. Occasionally, the magma rises to the Earth's surface and erupts, or bursts out, through cracks in the Earth's crust. The hot, liquid rock that erupts is called lava. Sometimes a volcanic eruption looks like a fiery fountain. Other

Sometimes lava moves like a river (RIGHT) and other times it sprays like a fountain (above).

times, the lava flows out of the Earth like a river.

When the lava cools and hardens, it turns into rock. Layers of lava build up after each eruption to form a volcano, also called a volcanic mountain. Some volcanoes form on dry land. Others form on the bottom of the ocean. Over time, the underwater volcanoes become mountainous islands—just like the Hawaiian Islands.

Maui, Island of Volcanoes

Maui began life as separate volcanoes. Over many thousands of years, wind and water eroded, or wore away, the lava on the tops and sides of the volcanoes. The loose rocks produced by this erosion were washed into a shallow sea channel between

Volcanoes created
the island of Maui.

the volcanoes. Eventually, the channel was filled in, connecting the volcanoes and forming the island of Maui.

Haleakalā is the larger of Maui's two volcanoes, towering 10,023 feet (3,056 meters) above the ocean. Over the years, Haleakalā's sharp peak was worn down by wind, water, and ice, leaving a huge bowl-shaped hole at its top. Many people call this hole a "crater," but it is actually a valley

The West Maui Mountains

created over time by erosion. The second volcano, West Maui, is much smaller. It stands 5,788 feet (1,765 m) above sea level. The West Maui volcano is lower because it is much older, and has been worn down by erosion.

The summit of Haleakalā is as rocky and barren as a desert. However, a tropical rain forest called Kīpahulu (key-pah-hoo-loo) Valley lies on its steep east slope. The

A woman walks through
a bamboo forest in the
Kīpahulu Valley.

valley is warm, wet, and filled with life. These areas are so special that the U.S. Congress included them as part of the Hawai'i National Parks in 1916, which later became the Hawai'i Volcanoes National Park. In 1960, Congress created Haleakalā National Park as a separate park for these special places. Haleakalā National Park was made an

International Biosphere
Preserve in 1980. A biosphere
is a natural life community, or
ecosystem, including animals,
plants, and the habitats that
support them.

Life in Haleakalā

Different kinds of plants and animals live in Maui's four life zones, depending on the area's altitude, or height above the sea. The mountain life zone is found on the high summit of Haleakalā. Way up there, the ground is rocky and dry. Days are hot and

Few plants or animals can survive at the top of Haleakalā.

nights are cold. Only a few hardy grasses and shrubs can grow there, and the only animals that live there are insects, spiders, and birds.

The bowl-shaped hole at Haleakalā is huge—7.5 miles (12 kilometers) long, 2.5 miles (4 km) wide, and more than 1/2 mile (1 km) deep. It has many "mini-volcanoes," or cinder cones, dotting its moon-like interior.

Cinder cones in the
"crater" at Haleakalā

ʻĀhinahina

The most unusual and loveliest of Haleakalā's mountain plants is the ʻĀhinahina (ah-hee-nah-hee-nah), or silversword. It is strong enough to grow in the wind, cold, heat, and drought of the summit. The plant's name means "moon-colored" and it has sharp, sword-like leaves covered with thick, silvery hairs. It blooms only once in its lifetime of about fifty years. Then it dies. During its brief bright bloom, the plant's stalk is covered with red blossoms.

A field of ferns growing
in the shrub land

Just below Haleakalā's
summit lies the shrub land. It
is wetter and milder than the
summit, so grasses and shrubs
grow well there. One of the

Nēnēs are only found in Hawai'i.

most unusual birds that lives there is the nēnē (NAH-nah)— the Hawaiian goose. The land-loving nēnē would rather walk than swim. But like all geese, the nēnē "honks" and flies.

Honeycreepers

Fifty kinds of Hawaiian honeycreepers are found in Hawai'i. One of the most beautiful is the 'i'iwi (EE-wee). This bright red bird has dark wings and white spots on its back. It sips nectar from wildflowers with its long curved bill.

Below the shrub land lie Haleakalā's two forest zones. Dry forest covers the southern and western slopes of Maui. A rain forest covers the northern and eastern slopes.

The Kīpahulu Valley, on the northeastern slope, receives up to 400 inches (1,000 centimeters) of rain a year. That's why the area is called a "rain forest." Many kinds of trees, plants, birds, and insects thrive in this tropical paradise. And

The Kīpahulu Valley is known for its forests and its waterfalls.

woven across Kīpahulu Valley, like a giant spider web, are beautiful mountain streams and rushing waterfalls.

The First People

About 1,600 years ago, a group of South Pacific islanders called Polynesians discovered the Hawaiian Islands. These ancestors of modern Hawaiians brought foreign plants with them, including sweet potatoes, sugar cane, and taro. They

Farmers still grow taro on Maui today.

also brought dogs, chickens, and pigs. Along with farming, Hawaiians have always fished, harvesting delicious foods from the rich waters around them.

In 1778, James Cook, an English sea captain, may have been the first European to see Hawai'i, which he named the Sandwich Islands. When other people from Europe came to Hawai'i in the early 1800s, they too brought

plants and animals—including rats, cattle, and later, a weasel-like predator called the mongoose. Soon, these new arrivals, along with runaway pigs, began destroying the native Hawaiian plants, animals, and birds. Today, less than two hundred years later, eighty-five kinds of birds have disappeared, and thirty-one others are endangered.

Haleakalā National Park was created, in part, to protect Maui's lovely landscapes and wildlife from further harm. That's why most of Haleakalā is a wilderness park, with few roads or services. But there are

One of the many trails for hikers
in Haleakalā National Park

plenty of hiking trails, and
walking is a lot more fun
than sitting in a car!

Visiting Haleakalā

Wherever you go in Haleakalā National Park, be prepared! The summit can be cold and cloudy at dawn and dusk, hot and sunny at midday, and very windy at any time. Lower down Haleakalā's slopes, expect rain.

To fully enjoy Haleakalā National Park, you must come

At the summit, the temperature changes greatly throughout the day.

prepared to walk—with good shoes, a sun hat, sunglasses, sunscreen, layered clothing, and plenty of water. Hiking trails loop throughout the park,

The park is filled with exciting paths for hikers.

except in upper Kīpahulu Valley, which is a biological reserve, where tourists are not allowed. You can see two amazing waterfalls if you take the Pīpīwai trail. The Kuloa Point loop trail will take you to the remains of a traditional Hawaiian village and several small waterfalls.

Like the Hawaiian god Maui, park visitors can watch the sun rise above Haleakalā. Popular viewpoints include the Haleakalā visitor center,

Sunrise at the park

the Kalahaku and Leleiwi
overlooks, and the summit.
Also, the sunset is superb from
the summit of Haleakalā, and
along the Halemau'u trail.

Fast Facts

Location: Haleakalā volcano covers about two-thirds of Maui, second largest of the eight major Hawaiian Islands. It lies in the Pacific Ocean, about 2,400 miles (3,860 kilometers) southwest of North America.

History: Haleakalā volcano is about 2 million years old. In 1916, Haleakalā became a national park of part of Hawai'i National Parks. In 1960, Haleakalā became its own park. In 1980, Haleakalā National Park was made an International Biosphere Preserve.

Size of park: 30,183 acres (12,215 hectares), including 19,270 acres (7,798 hectares) are wilderness.

Highest and Lowest points: Haleakalā National Park extends from sea level at Kukui Bay, to the summit of Haleakalā, 10,023 feet (3,056 meters) above the Pacific Ocean.

Climate: Haleakalā's summit is high, dry and desert-like, with hot days and cold nights. The farther you travel down Haleakalā's slopes, the wetter and warmer it becomes. The lush jungle of Kīpahulu Valley gets up to 400 inches (1,000 centimeters) of rainfall each year.

To Find Out More

Here are some additional resources to help you learn more about Hawai'i and Haleakalā National Park:

Books

Fradin, Dennis B. **Hawai'i.** Children's Press, 1996.

Nelson, Sharlene and Ted. **Hawaii Volcanoes National Park.** Children's Press, 1998.

Petersen, David. **National Parks.** Children's Press, 2001.

Organizations and Online Sites

Haleakalā National Park
P.O. Box 369
Makawao, HI 96768
http://www.nps.gov/hale

National Park Service
http://www.nps.gov/

This site contains official information on the National Park Service, with links to many national park and monument sites.

U. S. National Parks
http://www.US-national-parks.net/

This site offers links to all national parks where you can learn about the parks all around the United States and the ones near you.

Visiting Haleakalā
http://www.haleakala.national-park.com/

This site provides hiking, sightseeing, and visiting guides to Haleakalā National Park. There are also a number of photos of the park and a map of the area.

Important Words

altitude height above sea level

ancestor a relative who lived long ago

cinder volcanic ash and rock fragments

erode wear away

erupts throws out with great force

lava the hot liquid rock that pours out of a volcano when it erupts

predator an animal that kills other animals for food

summit the top

taro a tropical food plant whose root resembles a potato

tectonic plates the large slabs of rock that make up the Earth's crust

Index

(**Boldface** page numbers
  indicate illustrations.)

'Āhinahina, 26, **26**
altitude, 22
ancestor, 32
biosphere, 21, 43
cinder, 24, **25**
Cook, James, 34, **35**
erode, 14
erupts, 11
forest zones, 30, **31**
Haleakalā National Park
  animals and plants in,
    22–31
  fast facts, 43
  legend of, 5–8
  origin of, 20–21
  visiting, 38–42
Hawai'i, **4,** 8, 9–13, 32,
  34. See also Maui
  first people, 32, 34
  origin of islands, 9–13
hiking trails, 37, **37,** 39,
  40, 41–42

honeycreeper, 29, **29**
International Biosphere
  Preserve, 21, 43
Kīpahulu Valley, 18, **19,**
  30–31, **31,** 41
Kuloa Point, 41
lava, 10, 11, **12,** 13, 14
magma, 11
Māui (Hawaiian god), 5, 6,
  8, 41
Maui (island), **4,** 5, 14–21,
  22, 43
nēnē, 28, **28**
Polynesians, 32, 34
predator, 35, 46
rain forest, 18, 30
shrub land, 27, **27,** 30
summit, 22, 38, **39,** 42,
  43
taro, 32, **32**
tectonic plates, 10–11
volcanoes, 9–18, 43
West Maui Mountains,
  17, 18

Meet the Author

David Petersen credits his wife, Caroline, as the family expert on Haleakalā National Park, since she once lived on Maui. Today, Caroline and David live in a mountain cabin in Colorado. David enjoys researching and writing True Books, and has more than forty to his credit. David also writes "big kid's" books, mostly about nature, including *Ghost Grizzlies: Does the Great Bear Still Haunt Colorado?* (Boulder, Colo., Johnson Books, 1998).